JOURNEY WITH THE WISE MEN
DAILY READINGS FOR ADVENT

T0349774

JOURNEY WITH THE WISE MEN DAILY READINGS FOR ADVENT

Suitable for Every Calendar Year

Mathew Bartlett

Journey with the Wise Men by Mathew Bartlett

First Published in Great Britain in 2019.

FAITHBUILDERS

Bethany, 7 Park View, Freeholdland Road, Pontnewynydd, Pontypool NP4 8LP

www.faithbuilders.org.uk

British Library Cataloguing-in-Publication Data. A catalogue record for this book is available from the British Library

ISBN: 9781913181000

Cover Design by Faithbuilders. Cover Image © Rawpixelimages | Dreamstime.com

How to Use This Book

We've all heard of the star which guided the wise men to the infant Christ. But there were other signs which led them too, signs which indicated the existence and presence of the God and the king whom they sought. In these daily readings we discuss these in terms of:

Creation – Scripture – Miracle – Child

This book is designed for any year, and so does not contain dates, but rather lists "1st Sunday in Advent, 1st Monday, 1st Tuesday" etc.

Since Advent begins on a different date each year, and Christmas Day can fall on any day of the week, this guide begins on the first Sunday in Advent, and provides enough readings to last up to Christmas Day *whatever day it falls*. The suggested daily reading plan is separated into options for lectionary years A, B and C, and each reading has been chosen to compliment the usual lectionary readings for each year.

I do hope these readings will bless, strengthen and comfort you, and draw you nearer to seek our Lord at this most wonderful and blessed time. The wise men did not journey alone. The reader and author of these notes have probably never met, and we may be very different people, but we are all Christian believers journeying together with Christ.

9781913181000_txt.pdf 5   30/09/2019 12:02:51

Table for Advent 2019–2024

Advent 2019 A	Sunday, December 1, 2019	Tuesday, December 24, 2019
Advent 2020 B	Sunday, November 29, 2020	Thursday, December 24, 2020
Advent 2021 C	Sunday, November 28, 2021	Friday, December 24, 2021
Advent 2022 A	Sunday, November 27, 2022	Saturday, December 24, 2022
Advent 2023 B	Sunday, December 3, 2023	Sunday, December 24, 2023
Advent 2024 C	Sunday, December 1, 2024	Tuesday, December 24, 2024

9781913181000_txt.pdf 6

Introduction

There is no doubt that from the beginning of creation, people have looked to the stars to find inspiration and consider how their own place in the world contrasts with the greatness of the universe. To find a group of men in the scriptures – the so-called "three wise men" – who studied the stars is therefore no surprise. But who were these men, what was the "star in the East" (as the King James Version has it) which led them, and what significance did they attach to their journey to worship the infant Jesus?

The little we know about ancient astronomy is complicated by the fact we're not at all sure where in the world these learned men originally came from. It is generally supposed that they came from the areas around either Babylon or Persia (Iran and Iraq). Evidence for this supposition is very slim, but since the Jews had been in exile in both these centres, it might explain their seeming familiarity with at least some of the Old Testament scriptures. It may be that they were Chaldeans, as the Greeks later came to call astronomer-priests who not only made observations and mathematical predictions about heavenly objects, but frequently attached meanings to these events.

The three wise men were well educated in astronomy. Even if the average member of the population had failed to observe "his star in the East," these men did. How they came to take this as an omen of the birth of a king in Israel of such significance that they travelled long distances to worship him is unclear. One may speculate that from the writings of Daniel, and his study of scripture, some such omen was expected, and its nature predicted. I add here that unlike many scholars I believe Daniel to be a real figure of Jewish-Babylonian history and not a composite or fiction invented by an apocalyptic writer during the Hasmonean period.

Many theories have been proposed to account for the appearance of what the wise men called, "his star." I am attracted by the idea that it may have been an otherwise unrecorded nova or supernova in the Constellation of Aquila (or at least one for which records were lost).[1] This is said by some to have been observed by eastern astronomers in 5–4 BC, the year favoured

---

[1] http://articles.adsabs.harvard.edu/full/1978JRASC..72...65M

as the time of Christ's birth.[2] This would fit with a previous observation in 365 BC and the fact that Aquila contains binary stars.[3]

The observations concur with the star appearing to stand over Bethlehem (the azimuth of the supernova event suggests it could have been used by the wise men to navigate in this direction). Morehouse views it as a supernova rather than a nova, of considerable brightness, resulting in the formation of a pulsar (PSR 1913+16b to be precise).

A Journey from Astronomy to Faith in God?

Today we know far more about the universe than the three wise men could have known. For example, we know of stars which do not emit light, but rather radio waves, we know of galaxies beyond our own, and yet we have not reached the end of our exploration. We are still on our journey of knowledge. Einstein affirmed that we know less than 1% about anything!

Yet as reasoning beings, we humans continue to look beyond explanations of what exists, or even how things came to be. What fascinates us most is the question – why?

The Bible says that creation offers clear evidence of God's attributes, summing these up as "his eternal power and divine nature." The laws that keep the universe in place reveal the wisdom of the creator, and the knowledge of how these laws work is something still only fully known to him. The fact that he has placed us here on a stable planet that sustains our lives reveals his love and care for humanity. The notes affirm:

> The creation reveals so much about our creator and at the same time leaves us longing to know more. Hence the search, the reason for the journey. *(From the note for the first Sunday in Advent)*

It seems the wise men were in the first instance drawn to God through a recognition of his greatness in creation. They probably also had access to at least some of Israel's scriptures. Yet even for those who do not have a copy of the scriptures, the world around us and our own existence offer powerful evidence of God's reality.

> To offer a theist twist on the famous phrase of the philosopher, "I exist, therefore my maker exists." *(ibid)*

---

[2] See for example, http://keighleyastronomicalsociety.co.uk/the-star-of-bethlehem and https://ww w.bbc.co.uk/news/magazine-20730828
[3] https://www.universetoday.com/19592/aquila/

9781913181000_txt.pdf 8

This consciousness of God is an in-built aspect of our creation. According to Romans 1, it is only those who harden their hearts to deny such evidence that end up silencing the inner voice. This, writes Saint Paul, leaves us without excuse, which is another way of saying we are morally culpable before God.

Thus, in the worldview of the authors of scripture, atheism is not an intellectual difficulty but a moral one. Atheists are not enlightened by science but blinded by sin. They proudly announce that there is no voice of God for them to hear, whilst all the time they have shut their hearts to that constant, loving, wooing voice amplified across the universe.

At the beginning of Advent, we set out to accompany the wise men on their journey to Israel, then to Bethlehem, to the Christ child and to faith in God. We acknowledge that every journey must begin somewhere. However faint or strong our concept of God, we feel the need to explore, to engage with the big questions of life, and hopefully, find some answers. Or better still, we may even encounter the creator, and be content that he has the answers we need.

9781913181000_txt.pdf 9   30/09/2019 12:02:51

Week One: Creation

1st Sunday in Advent: *God Revealed Through Creation*

> *For since the creation of the world God's invisible qualities—his eternal power and divine nature—have been clearly seen, being understood from what has been made, so that people are without excuse. (Romans 1:20)*

One should not be surprised that men who studied the science of the stars were drawn to faith in God. When one contemplates the enormity of the universe, one is struck by the sense of awe which should generate worship. The minds of many intelligent people who survey the heavens conclude that creation represents a power beyond itself, a creative mind which can be explored, an infinity of possibilities in the universe.

> You do not see God, and yet you acknowledge him as God by his works. *(Cicero)*

With the advance of modern technology, we now know far more about the universe than these three ancient astronomers. And yet the depth and wonder we observe is even more amazing and deeply inspiring.

The Bible says that creation offers clear evidence of God's attributes, summing these up as "his eternal power and divine nature." The vast expanse of the universe declares God's greatness; the fixed laws which govern the heavenly bodies reveal his wisdom; and our place on this planet proves his love and care – for where else could our lives be sustained?

The creation reveals so much about our creator and at the same time leaves us longing to know more. Hence the search, the reason for the journey.

It could be that the wise men were initially drawn to God through a recognition of his greatness in creation. The world around us and our own existence offer powerful evidence of God's reality. To offer a theist twist on the famous phrase of the philosopher, "I exist, therefore my maker exists."

> **Prayer:** Lord, your work in creation fills us with wonder. The revelation you have given makes us want to know you more. As we begin the journey of Advent, help us to worship, and follow you, as the wise men did, on our personal journey of faith. Amen.

Reading Plan: Year A: Ps 122; Year B: Ps 80; Year C: Ps 25

9781913181000_txt.pdf 10

1st Monday: *The Heavens Declare the Glory of God*

> *The heavens declare the glory of God; the skies proclaim the work of his hands. Day after day they pour forth speech; night after night they reveal knowledge. They have no speech, they use no words; no sound is heard from them. Yet their voice goes out into all the earth, their words to the ends of the world. In the heavens God has pitched a tent for the sun. (Psalm 19:1–4)*

The only place in Scripture where we encounter the three wise men is in the Gospel of Matthew, and it seems quite important to Matthew that the wise men are not Jewish. They did not share the ancestral heritage of the people to whom God had revealed himself in the past. Nor did they necessarily have immediate access, as the Jews did through their priests and teachers, to God's voice in the Torah, Writings and Prophets. Yet David, perhaps the greatest of all Israel's kings, announces in today's reading (Psalm 19) that God has provided a universal, multilingual witness to his glory; a witness which is immediately available to every ethnic and language group in existence.

Even today, in the 21st century, there are some people groups whose languages have not been fully codified – and consequently many peoples who have yet to obtain a copy of the scriptures in their own language. Nevertheless, God has spoken to humanity in a language so clear that it requires neither words nor translation.

The witness of the heavens to God's glory (the perfection of his being and character) and his work (his power and ability to create) is a constant and unending message (*"day after day," "night after night"*).

Bible translators continue the painstaking work of bringing the gospel to all people in their own tongue. Yet the word which brought creation into being still speaks to all people. No wonder the last book of the Bible rejoices to record that the redeemed of the Lord in future glory come from *"every nation, tribe, people and language"* (Revelation 7:9).

> **Prayer:** Lord, we thank you for the witness of creation, which speaks to people from every nationality and language, drawing them to you. Help us your church to similarly bear witness of your glory and love throughout the whole world. In Jesus' name. Amen.

Reading Plan: Year A: Isa 2; Year B: Isa 64; Year C: Jer 33

9781913181000_txt.pdf 11

1st Tuesday: *The Camels are Coming!*

> *But ask the animals, and they will teach you, or the birds in the sky, and they will tell you; or speak to the earth, and it will teach you, or let the fish in the sea inform you. Which of all these does not know that the hand of the Lord has done this? In his hand is the life of every creature and the breath of all mankind. (Job 12:7–10)*

Have you ever wondered *how* the wise men travelled to Jerusalem from the east? It is doubtful, for security and other practical reasons, that they would have travelled alone. There may have been many servants in their retinue, and no doubt burden-bearing beasts, such as donkeys and camels. I chuckled as I thought to myself, did the camels know where they were going and who they were going to see?

Of course, it is unlikely that the animals and birds share the same sense of God that humans are capable of, for humans are created in God's image like no other creature. People can reason, speak, and commune with God. The attribution of human traits to animals should never be taken literally. Nevertheless, their existence and attributes teach us a lot about God.

The Bible frequently uses animals in parabolic fashion to describe the attributes of humans. In Isaiah 1, Judah is compared unfavourably with an ass, who knows the hand who feeds it, whereas the people of God had turned their backs on him. In Numbers, Balaam's donkey spoke to rebuke the prophet's lust for money. In our journey of faith, we must not ignore the witness of the animal creation to the wisdom and goodness of God.

How might animals express their joy that Christ their creator had come among them? His birth spoke of the original perfection in which they shared and the promise of its restoration. Did they appreciate Christ's coming as evidence of God's care? Jesus said not one sparrow falls to the ground, *"without your Father's care"* (Matthew 10:29). Did the camels recognise the creator in the manger of Bethlehem? I'd like to think that if they did, they would have responded to him as the source and goal of their life. So, do you really want to be outdone by a camel this Christmas?

> **Prayer:** Lord, we praise you that in wisdom you created the entire animal kingdom. Grant that we may study each species, to protect and learn from them as you intend. In Jesus' name. Amen.

Reading Plan: Year A: Rom 13; Year B: 1 Cor 1; Year C: 1 Thess 3

9781913181000_txt.pdf 12

1st Wednesday: *Don't be Hard of Hearing*

> *Do you not know? Have you not heard? Has it not been told you from the beginning? Have you not understood since the earth was founded? (Isaiah 40:21)*

We may wonder today why the wise men would make so much of their encounter with God through creation that it drew them to take a long journey, seeking God's promised king with all their hearts. Does creation still speak as powerfully to us today as it did to them so many years ago?

I must admit, I found it very frustrating when a close friend began to lose his hearing. He would tell me to speak up, so I would tell him to put his hearing aid in! My frustration stems in part from my own impatience, but also because I have had significant surgery on my vocal cords, which means it's as difficult for me to speak up as it is for him to hear!

This is the picture behind today's verse, from the beginning of the world, God's creation has spoken, giving consistent witness to his majesty, power and love. His voice has never been quiet; it is our hearing that has become dull! This happens when we harden our hearts to God's voice, or refuse to believe the witness of creation, or if we simply have our head buried so deeply in life's affairs that we lose sight of the beautiful world around us.

The rhetorical *"do you not know? Have you not heard?"* in Isaiah 40:21 reminds us of the words of Saint Paul in Romans 1:20, *"they are without excuse,"* – yes of course they have heard!

Don't be hard of hearing! Take a look at the glory of the world around you, the beauty of the flower and the glory of the stars. Dare to lift up your heart in awe, and let your awe turn to praise. If you describe yourself as atheist dare for a moment to be agnostic! If you are agnostic, dare for a moment to be still and know that he is God. Wherever you are on your journey of faith, don't ignore the voice of God. He is still speaking loud and clear!

> **Prayer:** Lord, thank you that you speak clearly to us in ways that we can easily understand. Forgive us for the times when we have been too busy to stop and listen to your voice. Let us hear your voice speaking through your Son Jesus Christ throughout this Advent season. Amen.

Reading Plan: Year A: Matt 24; Year B: Mark 13; Year C: Luke 21

9781913181000_txt.pdf 13

1st Thursday: *Love to Guide Us*

> *"Yet he has not left himself without testimony: He has shown kindness by giving you rain from heaven and crops in their seasons; he provides you with plenty of food and fills your hearts with joy." (Acts 14:17)*

The world around us does not simply bear witness to God's creative power; Romans 1 says it displays all his attributes. Since God is love (1 John 4:8) we should expect to find evidence of this. God's love may be observed in the whole creation. Not only did God say, when he completed creation, that *"it is good,"* we can see for ourselves that it is good for us!

Preaching to a crowd at Lystra in Acts 14, Paul referred to the basic supply of water and fertile soil, essential to the agrarian culture of the Greeks, and declared God's provision of the harvest to be evidence of his love, kindness and goodness. For Paul, the simple joy of living was a powerful sign that God had created us that he might do us good and make us happy.

The Christmas carol, "As with gladness men of old," takes its cue from Matthew 2:10, for when the wise men relocated the star, *"they were overjoyed"* to know that they were nearing the goal of their search.

We too can rejoice, for there is still good in the world. The vices of humanity, the violence and lust for pleasure, wealth, and power never fully succeed in destroying all good, and can never drown out the loving voice of the Lord (even if from time to time he must act in judgment against sin).

Paul's argument from natural theology is a sound one. The world is good, so its maker must be good. The earth provides our needs, and so our maker must have lovingly thought of us when he designed it. The God whom the wise men sought, who patiently awaited their arrival in Bethlehem, was kind and loving, and this drew their hearts to him. A capricious God would drive people away, but because our God is love, he draws us to himself: *"The Lord appeared to us in the past, saying: 'I have loved you with an everlasting love; I have drawn you with unfailing kindness.'" (Jeremiah 31:3)*

> **Prayer:** Lord we come to you to praise you for your loving kindness. Prepare our hearts afresh to kneel both at your manger and your throne, and worship you for your unending love, most clearly revealed to us in your Son Jesus. Amen.

Reading Plan: Year A: Ps 9; Year B: Ps 25; Year C: Ps 44

9781913181000_txt.pdf 14

1st Friday: *God Knows Us Inside and Out*

For you created my inmost being; you knit me together in my mother's womb. (Psalm 139:13)

The reading for today tells of the most intimate witness God has given to humanity. The bond between a mother and infant is one of the strongest in creation, for the unborn child and the newborn baby are completely dependent on their mother for everything.

Yet there is a bond stronger than that between a mother and baby, and that is the bond between the unborn child and his/her creator. The process of procreation, from conception to birth, still provides many challenges for the scientific and medical community. But the God who set this process in motion takes a personal interest in every child long before they are born.

Two things are in view here. The second part, "*you knit me together,*" may be a reference to the infant's body, but, "*you created my inmost being,*" is a reference to what we call the soul, the self-consciousness inherent in very human being which makes them cognisant of themselves, the world around, and of God.

According to the Bible we are all aware of the existence of God. The desire to seek God is an intrinsic part of our humanity. Many people today, even without the revelation of scripture, seek God in a wide variety of religious expressions. The wise men, led by the light of creation without, the witness of creation within, and the added knowledge which the scriptures gave them, headed to Bethlehem to meet their infant creator.

The God who appeared to humanity as a baby in a manger knew these wise men inside out. He knew all about their lives, their thoughts and feelings (John 2:24–25). He knew the way to connect with them, through the appearance of a new star in the heavens. And he knows all about you too. And he cares. Every individual is different, and God knows how to connect with each of us so that he may draw us closer to him in the journey of faith.

> **Prayer:** Lord, thank you that even before we were born, you loved us and knew us inside out. We praise you that you deal with each of us as individuals and support us through your all-knowledge. You understand our thoughts and everything which affects our lives. In Jesus' name. Amen.

Reading Plan: Year A: Isa 52; Year B: Isa 1; Year C: Joel 2

9781913181000_txt.pdf 15   30/09/2019 12:02:52

1st Saturday: *Freedom and Glory*

> *For the creation waits in eager expectation for the children of God to be revealed. For the creation was subjected to frustration, not by its own choice, but by the will of the one who subjected it, in hope that the creation itself will be liberated from its bondage to decay and brought into the freedom and glory of the children of God. (Romans 8:19–21)*

As we end this first week of Advent, we have considered the way in which the testimony of creation drew the wise men to seek for God. Today's verse explains that God's king was born to redeem and liberate creation.

In the Bible's overarching story, the good creation became cursed because of Adam's sin. But God, to redeem his creation from this curse, became flesh and was born as a baby (Jesus) in Bethlehem. Since the scripture had announced in advance that, *"cursed is everyone that is hanged on a tree,"* (Galatians 3:13) so the adult Jesus became sin for us, that he might nail our sin with his body to the cross. By this action he removed the curse from humanity, and so necessarily liberated all creation, which had been bound under the same curse. The Bible further says that this liberation will only be fully realised when Jesus returns to reign in glory on the earth.

What a wonderful future God has in store for creation! When Jesus returns, it will be restored to its original glory, and the lion dwelling with the lamb will be no mere picture, but an incredible reality. Several recent books have highlighted the blessings God has in store for this world when it is renewed. I fully share their view. However, as much as I believe that the present creation will be redeemed, I believe more than that.

As beautiful as the redeemed earth will be when Christ lifts the curse, one thousand years of earthly blessing will be followed by eternity in a new heaven and earth. The latter may be distinguished from the former in that there is no more sea, and no light from sun or moon, or any stars. Whereas the reign of Christ on earth is given a duration (a thousand years), our life in the new heaven and earth has no such limit (forever and ever). Rather than press the issue, I simply wish to encourage the reader that whatever the finer details of what God has planned for us – it will be glorious.

> **Prayer:** Lord, we thank you that, "the sufferings of this present time are not worthy to be compared with the glory which shall be revealed in us." In Jesus' name. Amen.

Reading Plan: Year A: Matt 24; Year B: Mat 21; Year C: John 3

Week 2: Scripture

2nd Sunday in Advent: *Guided by God*

> *I see him, but not now; I behold him, but not near. A star will come out of Jacob; a scepter will rise out of Israel. He will crush the foreheads of Moab, the skulls of all the people of Sheth. (Numbers 24:17)*

Although the desire in the hearts of the wise men to seek God may have begun when they witnessed the testimony of creation, the omen of the new star (nova) seems to have sent them looking for answers in Israel's scriptures. If indeed the wise men were Chaldeans, then they had some historical advantage, because of Judah's exile to Babylon the Jewish scriptures would have been readily available in their own country and language. Indeed, Daniel and Ezra were originally written in Aramaic, the lingua franca of Babylon, and the Babylonian Targum (Aramaic translations of the Hebrew Scriptures) were available.

What led the wise men to turn to the scriptures of Israel, and no other text? The answer may be that when they took readings of the nova in the sky, they discovered following its azimuth angle would lead them directly to the land of Judea.

So which scriptures might the wise men have referenced to form their understanding of the significance of the nova?

Perhaps they felt that the appearance of the star correlated with the messianic text of Numbers 24:17, where the metaphorical star is a reference to a king of Israel. It would not be too much to suppose that if the wise men had found this prophecy, would have linked the appearance of the nova with the coming of the long-awaited Messiah-king of the Jews. Clearly, since the prophets spoke often of the coming anointed son of David, if the wise men became conversant with Israel's scriptures, they would have known the Messiah was more than just another king. They may well have developed an understanding of the significance of his birth, in terms of the blessing God intended to bring to all peoples through him.

> **Prayer:** God our Father, we thank you that when we are unable to find direction and meaning in life, we will surely find it in your Word, the scriptures, which guide us more surely than any star. In Jesus' name. Amen.

Reading Plan: Year A: Ps 72; Year B: Ps 85; Year C: Ps 75

9781913181000_txt.pdf 17   30/09/2019 12:02:52

2nd Monday: *Kings Bearing Gifts*

> *May the kings of Tarshish and of distant shores bring tribute to him. May the kings of Sheba and Seba present him gifts. May all kings bow down to him and all nations serve him ... May gold from Sheba be given him. ... all nations will be blessed through him. (Psalm 72:10–11, 15, 17)*

Since the wise men had access to the scriptures which taught that the Messiah would bring blessing to all nations (e.g. Gen 22:18; Ps 72:17) they may have understood that non-Jews would be welcomed to worship the God of Israel. This would have encouraged them to make their journey. Scriptures like the one above, however, have also led many to speculate whether these wise men were themselves of royal blood. Psalm 72 predicts that kings of distant lands would bring gifts to the messianic ruler of Israel. This is the reason why the "three wise men" are also sometimes called "three kings." So, whereas we cannot be sure they were royal, we can see the reasons which have caused scholars over the centuries to suppose they were. Not to mention their audience with Herod – not something which would be granted to a commoner!

Similarly, the vicar's Christmas chestnut that the three gifts have symbolic meaning also finds its origin in a certain reading of the scriptures. *Gold* was always a suitable tribute *for a king*, but in Psalm 72 it is predicted that the foreign kings would bring gold to Israel's king. *Frankincense* was a staple of temple life *for the worship of God* in Solomon's day (1 Kings 10:2, 25; 1 Chron 9:29; 2 Chron 9:24; Neh 13:5, 9). Did the wise men envisage that under the new king, the glory of the reign of Solomon would be restored, as predicted by Isaiah?

Psalm 45:8 speaks of the king's robes being fragrant with *myrrh*, making this another suitable gift for a king. The symbolic link preachers make is that myrrh is *for the day of death*, since Jesus's burial linen was also soaked in myrrh and aloes (John 19:39). Perhaps Saint Paul has this in mind when he wrote that the risen Christ brings the hope of eternal life, the good news which spreads *"the aroma of Christ ... brings life"* (2 Corinthians 2:14–16).

> **Prayer:** Lord, as we approach your throne during this Advent season, we have no gold, frankincense or myrrh to bring, but we praise you that you will accept the love of our hearts. Amen.

Reading Plan: Year A: Isa 11; Year B: Isa 40; Year C: Zeph 3

2nd Tuesday: *God's Word is a Lamp*

> *But you, Bethlehem Ephrathah, though you are small among the clans of Judah, out of you will come for me one who will be ruler over Israel, whose origins are from of old, from ancient times. (Micah 5:2)*

Matthew makes clear that the wise men's knowledge of the scriptures was limited. They seem unaware of Micah's prophecy that the Messiah, David's descendant, would be born in David's hometown of Bethlehem. Herod's religious advisers convey this information, which he surreptitiously passes on. So although the wise men had been guided by the star, the star may have disappeared from view. Once again, they needed to turn to God's word.

There may have been several reasons why the star may have temporarily vanished, only to reappear again later. I guess cloudy skies would be the most obvious reason, but if the star was a nova, these have a habit of flaring up brightly at first, then reducing in radiance before borrowing material from a neighbouring star which causes another flare up. When God's word pointed them in the right direction, the star reappeared in such a way that now they could read the direction to Bethlehem and find the house where the young child was. No wonder they rejoiced!

Elsewhere in the New Testament, Saint Peter refers to the scriptures as "*a light shining in a dark place*" (2 Peter 1:19). God's word is "*a lamp for my feet, a light on my path*" (Psalm 119).

How grateful we are that God has given us the inspired word of the scriptures. If we *only* had the witness of creation, we would be left with a great deal we could not explain. But God has chosen to reveal himself to us through this most precious and miraculous phenomenon called the Bible, which I believe was written at God's behest, for "*All Scripture is God-breathed and is useful for teaching, rebuking, correcting and training in righteousness*" (2 Timothy 3:16).

> **Prayer:** Lord, thank you for the holy scriptures, which lead us into all truth, and bring us to peace. This Advent we acknowledge that this is because they lead us to your holy Son Jesus, born for us at Christmas time. We bring you our adoration and praise in Jesus' name. Amen.

Reading Plan: Year A: Rom 15; Year B: 2 Pet 3; Year C: Phil 1

2nd Wednesday: *The Suffering of the Innocents*

> *A voice is heard in Ramah, weeping and great mourning, Rachel weeping for her children and refusing to be comforted, because they are no more. (Matthew 2:18)*

An unintended result of the wise men's visit to Herod was the slaughter of the innocent children, every boy under two in the region around Bethlehem, the region referred to by Jeremiah as Ramah. Rachel, favourite wife of Jacob, died during childbirth and was buried near Bethlehem (Genesis 35:19); hence the picture of her weeping for her children.

Herod is the archetype of those evil rulers who oppress their own people. He serves to contrast with Jesus, the Prince of Peace, who came to relieve the distress of those who lived in darkness and the shadow of death (see Isaiah 9:2).

Although the wise men were right to call him *"the king of the Jews,"* from the beginning of his life Jesus was identified with the poor lower classes of society. Hence the reason for Herod's indiscriminate murder of the children of the poor – he expected Jesus to be among them. The coming of the Messiah was foreshadowed by the life of King David. He too was born in Bethlehem, as the youngest and least of his brothers. Yet he too was chosen by God to lead his people.

Following his miraculous escape from Herod, Jesus' life remained one of humility, suffering, and rejection. When the adult Jesus later came to Jerusalem to be hailed as king of the Jews, he came meekly, riding a donkey. In teaching the people he spoke in simple terms by the roadside, the seaside, or the hillside. When he came to teach in the temple, he was arrested and handed over to the Romans by the temple authorities. Yes, he too would share in the suffering of the innocents – since that is what it would take to finally defeat the evil which fills the hearts of men like Herod.

> **Prayer:** Lord, we only need to turn on the news to discover that there are still evil people like Herod in the world, and that the evils of violence, greed and lust for power destroy the lives of innocents. But since you have given your innocent life to suffer for us, we have hope in your return, when all suffering will end, and evil will forever cease. Amen.

Reading Plan: Year A: Matt 3; Year B: Mark 1; Year C: Matt 11

9781913181000_txt.pdf 20

2ⁿᵈ Thursday: *The Kingdom of Peace*

> *For to us a child is born, to us a son is given, and the government will be on his shoulders. And he will be called Wonderful Counselor, Mighty God, Everlasting Father, Prince of Peace. Of the greatness of his government and peace there will be no end. He will reign on David's throne and over his kingdom, establishing and upholding it with justice and righteousness from that time on and forever. The zeal of the Lord Almighty will accomplish this. (Isaiah 9:6–7)*

If, as we have supposed, the wise men had access to the Babylonian Talmud of Isaiah, then their understanding of the birth of the king of the Jews would almost certainly have been influenced by this prophecy. Here the rightful claimant to David's throne is predicted to reign over all people (*"Of the greatness of his government and peace there will be no end"*) for all time (*"from that time on and forever"*). His greatness is praised, and from these verses support is taken for the Christian belief in the incarnation – the view that Jesus was, from his birth, more than a mere man. He was – and is – God manifest in the flesh, God with us (Isaiah 7:14).

It is doubtful that the wise men would have fully understood this – as it seems even the disciples of Jesus did not appreciate these things until after his resurrection. Even so, the wise men could not doubt the greatness of the promised king.

The wise men welcomed and celebrated the birth of Christ, whereas Herod rejected and opposed his coming. But Isaiah's vision assures us that Christ's kingdom would be set up despite all opposition, and would continue forever, for *"The zeal of the Lord Almighty will accomplish this."*

Through his death and resurrection, Christ's kingdom has now come. It is up to each individual whether they oppose it, or celebrate and receive it, but no one can ever overthrow it! Christ the king now reigns eternally on God's throne!

> **Prayer:** Lord, we thank you that the kingdom of God, your kingdom of peace, has begun and will never end. We pray that we may live each day in anticipation of the full manifestation of that kingdom, when there will at last be "peace on earth." In Jesus' name. Amen.

Reading Plan: Year A: Ps 11; Year B: Ps 40; Year C: Ps 76

21

30/09/2019 12:02:52

2nd Friday: *Good News for All Nations*

> *It is too small a thing for you to be my servant to restore the tribes of Jacob and bring back those of Israel I have kept. I will also make you a light for the Gentiles, that my salvation may reach to the ends of the earth. (Isaiah 49:6)*

God's purpose in the election of Abraham, and later the nation of Israel, had always been that through them he would bring blessing to all nations. Christ's mission was to bring the fulfilment of this promise to Abraham, Israel, and the world. God's blessing would now be for all people. Indeed, in today's verse, Isaiah predicts that it would be *"too small a thing"* for Christ to be merely a national saviour. The creator of the world would also be its redeemer, liberating the whole universe from *"its bondage to decay"* (Romans 8:21).

In a sense, the wise men are the firstfruits of the Gentiles, representative of all those who would come to Jesus after Pentecost. The star drew the wise men to Jesus, but it is Jesus who draws all people to God. He is *"a light for the Gentiles"* who brings God's salvation *"to the ends of the earth."*

As many of us will be busily involved in Christian worship and witness throughout the Christmas season, it is encouraging to know that Christ is still the light of the world. The scripture still acts as a guide to lead people to him, and whether we read and explain scripture to congregations in church or speak gently about our faith to friends over coffee, we are doing something wonderful. We are showing them the light who brings peace, love and salvation to all people. One thing we never have to worry about is: who should be told this good news?

Should we share it with refugees from other nations, demonstrating the divine compassion which lies behind the message? Should we share our faith respectfully with those of other religious backgrounds? Should we approach those with no faith and tell them the good news? Yes! There is nothing exclusive about the gospel. It is good news for all people, forever.

> **Prayer:** Lord, we thank you that your good news was given that it might bring great joy to all nations. We pray that during Advent we shall be unafraid and unashamed to share the good news of Jesus with all those whom you bring across our path. Amen.

Reading Plan: Year A: 1 Kgs 18; Year B: 1 Kgs 22; Year C: Amos 7

9781913181000_txt.pdf 22   30/09/2019 12:02:53

2nd Saturday: *King of the Jews or King of the Ages?*

> *He was given authority, glory and sovereign power; all nations and peoples of every language worshiped him. His dominion is an everlasting dominion that will not pass away, and his kingdom is one that will never be destroyed. (Daniel 7:14)*

When the wise men arrived at Herod's palace, they asked *"where is he who has been born king of the Jews?"* (Matthew 2:2). As we have already discussed, we cannot be entirely sure of what they understood by this title *"king of the Jews."* But if they had access to the Aramaic text of Daniel, then they may have understood something of the nature of his rule – that Jesus would never be replaced, that somehow his rule would be everlasting, and that it would not be over Jews only, but over all nations.

The vision given to Daniel in chapter 7 of the four beasts corresponds to his earlier vision in chapter 2 of the great statue. These visions predict the rise and fall of all the major empires that would dominate the Middle East, and therefore the land of Israel, for hundreds of years. And yet ultimately it is *"one like a son of man, coming with the clouds of heaven"* (Daniel 7:13), *"the rock cut out of a mountain, but not by human hands,"* (Daniel 2:44–45) who ends their rule and sets up God's kingdom on earth. This kingdom, ruled by the *"son of man"* would result in, *"all the kingdoms under heaven will be handed over to the holy people of the Most High"* (Daniel 7:27).

If the wise men understood these things, then their worship at Bethlehem signifies more than the polite welcome of a new monarch. It represents the surrender of their lives, their willingness to be ruled by God's king Jesus in God's kingdom. This Advent, we too can make the decision to surrender our lives to Jesus. We can offer him our worship and acknowledge our willingness to serve him. As we do, we will discover that his kingdom has already begun in our lives and will continue beyond this life in his everlasting kingdom.

> **Prayer:** Lord, help us to mirror the surrender and worship of the wise men in our own lives. As we bow to you this Advent, we acknowledge your right to rule, and we gladly invite you to rule in our lives so that we might serve you and humanity in your kingdom. In Jesus' name. Amen.

Reading Plan: Year A: John 1; Year B: Luke 1; Year C: Luke 3

Week 3: Miracle

3rd Sunday in Advent: *The Miracle in the Heavens*

After Jesus was born in Bethlehem in Judea, during the time of King Herod, Magi from the east came to Jerusalem and asked, "Where is the one who has been born king of the Jews? We saw his star when it rose and have come to worship him." (Matthew 2:1-2)

The miracle of the appearance of the star to the wise men is multi-faceted, and yet each aspect of the miracle reveals something of God's universal yet personal love and care. As modern astronomers are aware, the appearance of a nova (or possibly a supernova) is not unique – nor could one be persuaded that such natural phenomena should be described as miraculous. It is not the event itself, but the way in which it was made to serve God's purposes which seems miraculous.

The increase in brightness of this star coincided with the birth of Jesus. That may be coincidence enough. But the azimuth of the star also led the wise men to the location of Jesus's birth. The coincidence now becomes extraordinary. The appearance of the star does not appear to have drawn much comment from Jerusalem's leaders, yet these Chaldeans not only saw in it a portent, they also established (probably with reference to Israel's scriptures) that it signified the birth of the messianic king. God knew how to communicate his purposes to these men. No doubt in order to get a certain star in a certain constellation to flare at a certain time to speak to a certain group of educated men involved the most careful planning from the beginning of creation. All these circumstances combined make us think of the otherwise natural event as miraculous.

This miracle not only shows God's personal love for the wise men, for it shows his control over the minute details of great cosmic events. This indicates his love for all humanity. We have not been left to our own devices, to spin helplessly on this globe towards future extinction. We have a God whom we call Father, who has fixed the laws which govern the spiral galaxies, and who sees a little sparrow as it falls.

Prayer: Dear God, help us to realise, as we seek to do all we can to rescue our environment and preserve the earth's precious resources, that we are not alone; you also care for creation. Amen.

Reading Plan: Year A: Ps 146; Year B: Ps 126; Year C: Ps 50

24

3rd Monday: *The Miracle on Earth*

> *All this took place to fulfill what the Lord had said through the prophet: "The virgin will conceive and give birth to a son, and they will call him Immanuel" (which means "God with us"). (Matthew 1:22–23)*

Have you ever wondered, as I have, what the wise men learned when they spoke to Mary about the infant king? Did she tell them of the fulfilment of Isaiah's prophecy, that she was the virgin who had given birth? Did they know of the prophecies which stated this child would be more than a mere man – he would be *"God with us."*

When one considers the many miracles of Christmas (the star, the virgin conception, the message of Gabriel, the song of the angels to the shepherds, and the miraculous birth of John), perhaps this is the greatest miracle of all – that through Jesus God is with us.

The incarnation is a simple yet incredibly profound concept. God, who always was and is and is to come, came to the womb of a young virgin, and through the power of the Holy Spirit became the human existence of Jesus of Nazareth. This miraculous event has been the subject of endless discussion by scholars through the church age. Perhaps there is much we do not know but let us at least remind ourselves of what the scripture tells us about this extraordinary event.

Jesus was no ordinary man in whom God came to dwell. He was not somehow chosen to bear God's image in a unique way. No, the scripture is specific, *"the Word became flesh"* (John 1:14). The Word did not share the flesh of another – there is no division in the personality of Jesus. He is God, and he is man – as he was in Mary's womb, as he was in Bethlehem's manger, so he still is today. He is God with us.

> **Prayer:** Lord, as we face difficult and discouraging days, we are nevertheless filled with the joy at the assurance that you are with us and will remain with us through all of life's events. Thank you, we cannot manage without you. Amen.

Reading Plan: Year A: Isa 35; Year B: Isa 61; Year C: Isa 12

9781913181000_txt.pdf 25

3rd Tuesday: *The Miracle of Protection*

> *And having been warned in a dream not to go back to Herod, they returned to their country by another route. (Matthew 2:12)*

The wise men may have travelled with servants and a caravan of beasts of burden, but when trouble came they were hardly ready to take on Herod, who was supported by his army and backed by Rome as its puppet king. It is probably just as well that they were wide-eyed and innocent enough to take Herod at his word, or else he might not have let them get as far as Bethlehem.

But if our heroes were out-witted and out-manoeuvred by Herod, yet they were still perfectly secure. And how grateful we should be that we, the people of God, although unarmed and seemingly at the mercy of forces more powerful than us are nevertheless always under divine protection.

Indeed, like the wise men, we may frequently be unaware of the dangers which we face, or of the divine protection which covers us every day. God was aware of Herod's plans, and by means of dreams he warned both the wise men and Joseph to escape them. It may not seem like much, but it was enough to defeat the powerful tyrant.

Our God knows all things, even the thoughts which people try to hide in their hearts, the evil plans they make which they believe no one can see. And even if our opponents, like Herod, can call upon physical strength and the power of arms, God is still able to confound them. Like the wise men, we are safe not because of what we know, or the strength that we have, but because we are hidden and kept safe by God.

Prayer: Lord, we praise you that day by day we are kept safe from the plans of evil people. Although some wish to destroy your church, we remember that at worst, they can kill the body and after that can do no more. We thank you that even should we die in the service of our God, we are kept eternally secure in your love, and have the certain hope of resurrection to eternal life through Jesus Christ our Lord. Amen.

Reading Plan: Year A: John 5; Year B: Matt 14; Year C: Luke 4

9781913181000_txt.pdf 26

3rd Wednesday: *The Miracle of Timing*

> *But when the set time had fully come, God sent his Son, born of a woman, born under the law, to redeem those under the law, that we might receive adoption to sonship. (Galatians 4:4–5)*

As we read the Christmas story afresh, we cannot but be amazed that the appearance of this particular nova coincided with the birth of Christ in such a way that announced his coming to the world and led the wise men to him.

In the verse above from Galatians, we are reminded that God is not only in charge of the material universe, but of time itself. No one has power over the constellations so that they can decide when a star should begin to nova or supernova. No one, that is, except God.

"When the set time had fully come," which is to say, at the precise time God had chosen, he sent his son Jesus to the world. In the Gospels we read of the movement of an entire empire during the taxation of Augustus, which God further utilised to serve his purposes for the birth of Jesus.

Nothing is beyond God's control. So why do we worry? If God is so powerfully at work in the cosmos, and among the nations, then we ought not to doubt his *ability* to help us. If God is, as Jesus said, concerned with the tiny details of creation, so that not even a sparrow falls to the ground without our Father, then we cannot doubt his *availability* to help us. And if God so loved the world that he gave his only son Jesus, then we cannot doubt his *intention* to help us.

So whatever difficulties we may be experiencing in life right now, we can pause to think – God knew all about it and has long ago planned and promised to make his presence available to us through Jesus in every situation.

> **Prayer:** Lord, I admit that sometimes I pass through dark times when I cannot feel the presence or love of God. Thank you that at these times, you have promised to be there. Help us to accept your promise by faith, until we experience your presence and love without limit in heaven. In Jesus' name. Amen.

Reading Plan: Year A: James 5; Year B: 1 Thess 5; Year C: Phil 4

9781913181000_txt.pdf 27

3rd Thursday: *The Miracle of Family*

> *After Herod died, an angel of the Lord appeared in a dream to Joseph in Egypt and said, "Get up, take the child and his mother and go to the land of Israel, for those who were trying to take the child's life are dead." So he got up, took the child and his mother and went to the land of Israel. (Matthew 2:19–21)*

Throughout the Christmas story, although Jesus is proclaimed as the son of God, he is protected by the actions of his parents, especially Joseph, in obedience to God's instructions. At once we perceive why it was so important for Jesus to be born into a loving and supportive family.

Mary had proved her piety and faith following the annunciation by Gabriel that she would conceive in her virginity and give birth to the son of the highest. She had obeyed; *"May your word to me be fulfilled,"* she said (Luke 1:38). Joseph similarly proves his faith when God revealed to him the truth about Mary's conception and about the identity of the child to be born. Both parents have proven themselves faithful and obedient, and so were ready, with God's help, to care for the infant Jesus.

Becoming a parent for the first time is a wonderful experience but it can also be daunting. There is a precious new life, who completely depends on you for feeding, washing, dressing, and a host of other things. The weight of responsibility is very great. Thank God that as Christians we do not carry the burden alone. In the Christmas story, God is caring for his son, and Jesus later tells us about a God who is caring and concerned for every son, and every daughter, and every parent.

If I were asked for parenting advice, then at the top of my list for parents would be godliness. Since God cares for our families even more than we do, his instructions are surely in their best interests. It is good for us to be like Joseph, and obey God's commands in faith, knowing that it will bring blessing for our children.

> **Prayer:** We thank you, Lord, for every member of our families, and for our church family too. We pray for every parent during Advent. Grant them the wisdom and skill to bring up their children and provide for their needs. We pray that they shall feel the love God has for all his children – young and old. Amen.

Reading Plan: Year A: Ps 12; Year B: Ps 68; Year C: Ps 14

3rd Friday: *The Miracle of Justice*

> *But when he heard that Archelaus was reigning in Judea in place of his father Herod, he was afraid to go there. Having been warned in a dream, he withdrew to the district of Galilee, and he went and lived in a town called Nazareth. So was fulfilled what was said through the prophets, that he would be called a Nazarene. (Matthew 2:22–23)*

When the time came, Joseph was instructed by God to return to Israel with Mary and the child Jesus. We are not sure what age Jesus would have been at this time, but he was still a child. So, Herod had died not long after the slaughter of the innocents. I cannot help but think that God himself had been involved in the removal of Herod as an act of judgment.

Even so, it would still not be safe for the family in Judea. Archelaus would no doubt have known of the prophecy of a child born in Bethlehem and been urged by his father Herod to act against this threat to his throne. From the above verses we see the nature of God's guidance to Joseph. Initially, the guidance was simply to return to Israel, but as Joseph obeyed, he received more detailed guidance, which led him to Nazareth.

From this we can be sure that God is able to deliver his people from the injustice of evil rulers. There is no great pomp and display here of God's power; here is no repeat of the plagues of Egypt. But silently, revealing his word to his chosen ones, God is constantly at work, preserving the faithful and watching over the cause of justice, equity, and peace.

Evil rulers from that day until now have produced widespread suffering and injustice. Although Christians believe that all men are accountable to God, and that a future day of judgment is fixed, we are faced with the challenge of recognising God's call for justice here and now. Who will help today's refugees fleeing persecution at the hands of the latest "Herod?" Since God takes the side of justice, if we are willing to stand up for the oppressed communities of the world, we will find God at our side.

> **Prayer:** Lord, as you are constantly working for justice in this world, help us to be agents of justice. We pray for all those suffering as a result of the decisions of the powerful and look forward to the day when our king Jesus will reign in righteousness, and injustice and suffering will be no more. Amen.

Reading Plan: Year A: Isa 5; Year B: Mal 3; Year C: Isa 25

3rd Saturday: *The Miracle of Scripture's Fulfilment*

> *So was fulfilled what was said through the prophets, that he would be called a Nazarene. (Matthew 2:23)*

As we read through chapter 2 of Matthew's Gospel, we immediately notice the pattern of scriptural fulfilment which Matthew highlights: *"for this is what the prophet has written"* (v. 5) … *"And so was fulfilled what the Lord had said through the prophet"* (v. 15) … *"Then what was said through the prophet Jeremiah was fulfilled"* (v. 17) … *"So was fulfilled what was said through the prophets"* (v. 23).

In our home, there is a lot of preparation and planning involved in the celebration of Christmas. We will start to buy in a variety of foods, order gifts online, buy wrapping paper and so on, as early as October! Planning Advent and Christmas services in the churches where I work starts even earlier, perhaps a whole year in advance. We must plan how, where and when to get the family together for Christmas. In the United States, similar plans are made for Thanksgiving.

The coming of Jesus into the world had been planned long ago. The Old Testament prophets had spoken of him again and again from earliest times. The first promise in the Bible (Genesis 3:15) is taken by Christians to be a reference to Jesus. In fact, after his resurrection Jesus said to his disciples, *"Everything must be fulfilled that is written about me in the Law of Moses, the Prophets and the Psalms"* (Luke 24:44). Speaking to the Pharisees Jesus once declared *"Moses … wrote about me"* (John 5:46). Clearly, the coming of Jesus had been painstakingly prearranged.

Yet the plan itself went back even further than the days of the prophets. That Jesus would come into the world as God incarnate to die to redeem his people from their sins had been decided before the world was even created, before Adam took his first breath (see 1 Peter 1:20). God's loving, careful planning was for our sakes. In the coming of Jesus, all that planning was fulfilled.

> **Prayer:** Father God thank you for the planning and fulfilment of your loving plan to save us through Jesus Christ. Amen.

Reading Plan: Year A: Acts 13; Year B: Rom 5; Year C: 1 Cor 4

Week 4: The Child

4th Sunday in Advent: *The Child who Reveals God's Humility*

> *In your relationships with one another, have the same mindset as Christ Jesus: Who, being in very nature God, did not consider equality with God something to be used to his own advantage; rather, he made himself nothing by taking the very nature of a servant, being made in human likeness. And being found in appearance as a man, he humbled himself by becoming obedient to death—even death on a cross! (Philippians 2:5–8)*

As the wise men commenced their long journey, they expected to find a *"king of the Jews,"* but as their journey reached its climax, they arrived at a lowly stable, to a baby born in a small town to poor peasant parents. One wonders how the wise men came to reconcile this great difference between expectation and reality in their minds. Did they work out that the exalted God had become flesh to dwell among the poorest of people?

In the verses above, looking back after the events of Jesus's crucifixion and resurrection, Paul presents the fuller significance of Christ's lowly birth. Paul saw Jesus's humility as something intrinsic to his nature. God the son was humble by nature, for although he was God, he was not grasping for position and power. Those (like Lucifer) who were not as great as God might grasp to be like him, but Jesus had no such need. His humility flows from his greatness. One might say it was not an effort for Christ to humble himself, just as it was no effort for him to be who he was. The purpose for his coming was similarly not forced. Jesus as the son of God shared God's love for the world. His willingness to suffer and die to redeem humanity was not innovative – it was never in doubt. His perfect obedience to the Father stemmed from his love for God and was his delight not his chore. In every way, Jesus is the exalted king, not only of the Jews, but of glory and of heaven. Like Paul, as we worship this Christmas, we see no disconnection between Christ's glory and his being born in a lowly stable. This is the God we worship. This is our king. We are drawn not merely to admire his greatness, but to love him because he first loved us.

> **Prayer:** Lord Jesus, we stand in awe that as the God of power and might, you felt equally at home in heaven and the manger of Bethlehem. We praise you that your coming means that one day we will join you and worship you in glory. Amen.

Reading Plan: Year A: Ps 80; Year B: Ps 89; Year C: Ps 144

9781913181000_txt.pdf 31

4th Monday: *The Child who Reveals God's Majesty*

> *The Son is the radiance of God's glory and the exact representation of his being, sustaining all things by his powerful word. After he had provided purification for sins, he sat down at the right hand of the Majesty in heaven. (Hebrews 1:3)*

Although born in a lowly manger, brought up in a humble home, and remaining poor throughout his ministry, Jesus displayed a divine majesty wherever he went.

God's majesty or kingly nature is the sum total of his kingly attributes as ruler of the universe. It is revealed by his creative power, as in the above verse from Hebrews Jesus is credited with, *"sustaining all things by his powerful word."*

The writer to the Hebrews also tells us that, *"The Son is the radiance of God's glory and the exact representation of his being."* God's glory is a reference to his nature, which Jesus perfectly displays. In what ways does Jesus reveal his glory?

Through his willingness to share our humanity and poverty, Jesus revealed the lowly heart of God, who is high and lofty but dwells with the humble. In Isaiah 57:15 God says, *"I live in a high and holy place, but also with the one who is contrite and lowly in spirit, to revive the spirit of the lowly and to revive the heart of the contrite."*

Through his ability to deliver the demon possessed, heal the sick and raise the dead, Jesus revealed the power and compassion of God. Through his teaching of things hidden since the world began, Jesus revealed the wisdom of God. Through his death on the cross for our sins, Jesus revealed the forgiving nature and love of God. Through his rising from the dead Jesus revealed the unending nature of the life of God.

In every way, Jesus reveals the glorious nature and majesty of the Father.

> **Prayer:** Lord Jesus, we praise you that you are the exact representation of the Father's love, power, and goodness. You reveal every aspect of God's nature to us, and we worship you for your radiant majesty. Amen.

Reading Plan: Year A: Isa 7; Year B: 2 Sam 7; Year C: Micah 5

9781913181000_txt.pdf 32

4th Tuesday: *The Child who Reveals God's Glory*

> *For in Christ all the fullness of the Deity lives in bodily form, and in Christ you have been brought to fullness. He is the head over every power and authority. (Colossians 2:9–10)*

It is as true today as it was two thousand years ago, that not everyone recognises Jesus as the unique person who reveals the glory of God. The wise men had recognised him as king of the Jews, but we are not sure what more they learned about Jesus from Mary and Joseph. When we consider the few people to whom God revealed the identity of the baby born in Bethlehem, it is hardly surprising that he remained in obscurity. The glory of the incarnate God was still veiled by his humanity – he looked like any other boy.

It was thirty or so years later that the veil was temporarily removed and the glory of God, "*the fullness of the Deity*," was allowed to shine out. This event was witnessed by Peter, James, and John on the mount of transfiguration. About this occasion, John wrote, "*We have seen his glory, the glory of the one and only Son, who came from the Father*" (John 1:14). Peter similarly reminisced, "*He received honor and glory from God the Father when the voice came to him from the Majestic Glory, saying, 'This is my Son, whom I love; with him I am well pleased.'*" (2 Peter 1:17).

Following his death and resurrection, Christ returned to his position in eternal glory with his Father. The scripture is very clear that he will one day return from there in power and glory to rule the earth (e.g. Matthew 16:27; 24:30; 25:31).

Although we cannot now see his glory, we can still contemplate the glory of God as it has been revealed in Jesus (see 2 Corinthians 4:6). This is the way we can make progress in our spiritual journey. And although the world in general still fails to recognise him, the time will come when every eye shall see him and recognise the glory of God in the face of Jesus Christ.

> **Prayer:** Lord, we so long for all the world to recognise your glory and worship you as the son of the Father. The thought of your coming again motivates us to proclaim your praise, so that others may also look forward to the day of your glorious return. Amen.

Reading Plan: Year A: Rom 1; Year B: Rom 16; Year C: Heb 10

9781913181000_txt.pdf 33

30/09/2019 12:02:54

4th Wednesday: *The Child who Reveals God's Grace*

> *The Word became flesh and made his dwelling among us. We have seen his glory, the glory of the one and only Son, who came from the Father, full of grace and truth. (John 1:14)*

The claim of the wise men was, "*We saw his star when it rose,*" and they rejoiced to eventually find and worship the infant king. But later believers were privileged to hear Jesus teach, see him perform miracles, and touch him after he had risen from the dead. They came to believe that he was God manifest in the flesh, and it is in this context that Saint John writes, "*we have seen his glory.*"

John offers a further description of that glory when he says that Christ's glory is "*full of grace and truth,*" and contrasts this directly with previous revelation: "*For the law was given through Moses; grace and truth came through Jesus Christ*" (John 1:17). The law given through Moses condemned people as sinners, but did not offer them the power to meet God's righteous requirements for living. But when Jesus came, he not only fulfilled the law himself, he also made forgiveness available to all who had broken God's laws. In addition to this, he gives the empowerment of a new spiritual birth to all who believe in him so that they might live to please God.

Grace is unmerited favour. Although God is all-powerful, he is not a tyrant. People may submit to a tyrant in fear of terrible punishments for disobedience. But the glory of Christ is such that men and women flock to him, for he heals their broken hearts, mends their broken lives, and forgives the brokenness of their moral characters.

At Christmas time, and all year round, the glory of our king Jesus is revealed most clearly by the fact that he, "*welcomes sinners and eats with them,*" and completely forgives their sins.

> **Prayer:** Lord, we praise you that you came into this world to reveal God's grace. We thank you for your love which has drawn us to you, forgiven our sins, and given us the empowering fresh start of new birth. Help us at this busy and stressful time of year to show others the same kindness and grace we have received from you. In Jesus' name. Amen.

Reading Plan: Year A: Matt 1; Year B: Matt 2; Year C: Luke 2

4th Thursday: *The Child who Reveals God's Power*

> *For in him all things were created: things in heaven and on earth, visible and invisible, whether thrones or powers or rulers or authorities; all things have been created through him and for him. He is before all things, and in him all things hold together. (Colossians 1:16–17)*

This Advent we have already discussed the creative power of the God who put the stars in space, and who at just the right time ordained for one to go into nova. The above verses from Colossians underline that not only was Christ involved as the agent of this creative process ("all things were made *by* him") but also that he was the focus of this process ("all things were created *for* him"). Even the invisible world was created for him – for it is Christ who made the angels and spiritual powers of this world, and these were created to serve him.

Christ is *before all things* not only in terms of his eternal existence, but also in terms of his priority. There is no higher name than the name of Jesus. It is the most exalted name in the universe. Jesus said that, "*All authority in heaven and on earth has been given to me*" (Matthew 28:18). Because he is victorious over sin, death, and hell, God, "*exalted him to the highest place and gave him the name that is above every name, that at the name of Jesus every knee should bow, in heaven and on earth and under the earth, and every tongue acknowledge that Jesus Christ is Lord, to the glory of God the Father*" (Philippians 2:10). There is no angel who can claim his throne, no higher power to whom he must bow.

In this way Jesus reveals God's own power and authority over all things. He is God's viceroy, wielding all of God's power on his behalf. The supreme way in which he shows that power is by his absolution of sinners. Consider the power than can take a child of the devil and make him or her a child of God! It is the power that can make a sinner a saint, and an enemy a friend. Perhaps for someone reading this, God's power can turn the unhappiness of their lives into a joyful celebration of the Saviours birth. Happy Christmas.

> **Prayer:** We thank you, Lord, for your power which keeps the universe in order, and which can bring order, love, peace and joy into our lives, no matter how cruel or chaotic the world around us may be. In Jesus's name. Amen.

Reading Plan: Year A: Ps 113; Year B: Ps 131; Year C: Ps 123

9781913181000_txt.pdf 35

4th Friday: *The Child who Reveals God's Love*

> *For God so loved the world that he gave his one and only Son, that whoever believes in him shall not perish but have eternal life. (John 3:16)*

Today's verse is perhaps the best-known of all Bible verses. I recall reading that this sentence has been translated into more languages and dialects than any other piece of literature. And no wonder, for it conveys the most important information for the whole world. Whoever, wherever, whenever you are – you are loved. Whatever your race, colour, religion, gender, state of mind, or state of health, you are loved. To be specific, you are loved by God. If we have been fortunate enough to experience human love, we can begin to realise how much greater God's love must be.

God's love is not sentimental, but practical. He did not send us emotional love songs from heaven to make us weep. He took decisive action to rescue us from our sins and their eternal consequences. By sending his son Jesus he demonstrated his love. As Jesus carried his Father's plan for our rescue through to completion, we realise how much it cost him. *"God demonstrates his own love for us in this: While we were still sinners, Christ died for us."* (Romans 5:8)

Jesus gave up his own perfect, sinless life on our behalf, to redeem us from our sin. God's purpose, according to John 3:16, is that we *"shall not perish."* The stakes were really that high. To be eternally lost, subject to the everlasting punishment which sin merits – that is what Jesus came to save us from. But Jesus' death not only rescues us from a terrible fate, it brings us to a wonderful destiny, *"but have eternal life."*

The reason Christmas warms our hearts is that it is truly a celebration of love. Many people say the festival has become too commercialised. Few of us can doubt that. Yet, so long as we can avoid the infection of materialism for its own sake, we are nevertheless right to express our love by the giving of gifts. *"For God so loves the world that he gave...."* Love must give. And the response to the gift must also be love. This Christmas let us remember to love God, for he first loved us and sent his son.

> **Prayer:** Lord, we thank you that you have shown great love for us by giving us your only Son. So we will give our love to you in return and look for opportunities to show our love for others in practical ways. Amen.

Reading Plan: Year A: 1 Sam 1; Year B: Zech 2; Year C: Isa 10

9781913181000_txt.pdf 36   30/09/2019 12:02:54

Christmas Day: *The Child who Reveals God's Salvation*

> *Salvation is found in no one else, for there is no other name under heaven given to mankind by which we must be saved. (Acts 4:12)*

Christmas Day has finally arrived. Like the wise men, we come to the end of our Advent journey on Christmas Day and celebrate Christ's birth. However, I am sure the wise men discovered that the end of their search was simply the beginning of a relationship that would last beyond this life to the next.

Similarly, although our Christian lives revolve around holy days such as Christmas and Easter, they are not limited to these. Jesus came to live among us every day of the year, and he is here still. Our responsibility is to live for him every day.

And that includes today! Many of us will be busy. Some of us will be working today, perhaps in essential services or catering. Some of us will be taking services of celebration and thanksgiving in our churches today and will need this advice more than most. For leading public worship, and expressing our deep inmost worship, are not always the same thing. Whatever our role today, we need time to reflect on our relationship with God. That is why we come apart for a moment, before the responsibilities of work or religious service, before presents are opened, before the family meal is cooked served and dishes washed, or friends taken to the local restaurant for a Christmas Day meal. Take time to read from God's word, pray, and worship from the heart.

Salvation is not just the experience we have when we first welcome Christ into our lives. Through faith in Jesus we were born again, but a new-born child needs his/her parent every day! Salvation is a journey which we have begun with God, and he expects us to keep in constant contact with him.

On this Christmas Day as any other day, we can be sure of God's presence with us as we walk with him on our earthly pilgrimage, each step of the way and in everything we do.

> **Prayer:** Lord, we praise you for your salvation. By your grace we have finished our journey *to you* and begun a fresh journey *with you*, knowing that you will walk with us and bring us safely to your heavenly and eternal kingdom. In Jesus' name. Amen.

Reading Plan: Year A: Rev 22; Year B: Rev 21; Year C: Rev 1

9781913181000_txt.pdf 37